THE GRIZZLY

BY
JEROLYN ANN NENTL

EDITED BY
DR. HOWARD SCHROEDER
Professor in Reading and Language Arts
Dept. of Elementary Education
Mankato State University

E. C. I. A.
Chapter II

PRODUCED AND DESIGNED BY
BAKER STREET PRODUCTIONS
Mankato, MN

CRESTWOOD HOUSE
Mankato, Minnesota

LIBRARY OF CONGRESS CATALOGING IN PUBLICATION DATA

Nentl, Jerolyn Ann.
   The grizzly.

(Wildlife, habits and habitat)
   SUMMARY: Discusses the powerful North American bear: where and how he lives, what he looks like, and what is to become of him.
   1. Grizzly bear--Juvenile literature. (1. Grizzly bear. 2. Bears) I. Schroeder, Howard. II. Title. III. Series: Widlife, habits and habitat.
QL737.C27N46   1984   599.74'446   83-22354
ISBN 0-89686-245-3 (lib. bdg.)

International Standard Book Number:	Library of Congress Catalog Card Number:
Library Binding 0-89686-245-3	83-22354

CRESTWOOD HOUSE

Hwy. 66 South, Box 3427
Mankato, MN 56002-3427

TABLE OF CONTENTS

INTRODUCTION:

"I hope we see a bear," Steven wished out loud as he put another sleeping bag into the car.

"I don't want to get too close to one," Susan said as she handed him one of their backpacks. "I hear that they're all over the place. They come right up to your car begging for food."

"I think only black bears do that," Steven said stopping to wipe the sweat from his face. It was just ten o'clock in the morning, but the sun was bright and it was already getting hot. Steven and Susan had intended to leave on their vacation earlier that morning. Instead, they had stayed up late the night before getting their things ready. They were headed for Yellowstone National Park. For two weeks they were going to camp and hike in the back country. The trip had been planned for a long time. They had read as much as they could about the Park and the wildlife there. They had sent for information from the Park and the states around it. They had wanted to learn as much as they could before their visit.

"The black bears beg for food all the time in the Park," said Steven. He had been thinking about all he had read on bears in the last few months. "However, you don't often find a grizzly where humans are, so you seldom see them begging for food. They live as far back in the mountains as they can get. They want to be left alone."

"I thought grizzly bears attacked people," Susan replied. "I heard about a man being killed right in his sleeping bag by a grizzly bear."

"That's true," Steven said. "Grizzly bears are very unpredictable. The most dangerous ones are those that have lost their fear of people. What's worse, is that some people have lost their fear of bears. They try to get too close to take a picture of them or feed them."

The grizzly bear is very unpredictable.

"Well, I'm not scared of them, but I will respect them," Susan said. "I just want to understand the facts so I'll know what to do if I come across one."

"The main thing is to stay out of their way. If you know their habits at different times of the year, you can avoid them," Steven said. "This time of year they should be a lot higher in the mountains than we will be, so we shouldn't have any trouble."

"I still hope I get a look at a grizzly, though," Steven sighed. "But I'll be content to watch it from a distance. Did you pack my field glasses?"

It's best to use field glasses, and watch grizzlies from a distance.

CHAPTER ONE:

The grizzly once lived all across North America

Most people will never see a grizzly bear except in a zoo. This brown bear now lives only in the most rugged wilderness areas of North America where few people are able to go.

It was not always this way. The grizzly bear once lived across most of this continent. The land was still wild and unsettled at that time. Grizzly bears roamed the mountains and the prairies searching for food. They curled up to sleep wherever they could find a good place. The grizzly was king of the land. It was the fiercest, most powerful animal. It could bring down a buffalo with one swipe of its powerful paw. It could carry off the carcass of a one-thousand pound elk. No other animal could prey upon the grizzly.

At one time it was thought that there were more than eighty species, or kinds, of these large brown bears. Now scientists know that there is only one — the brown bear they call *Ursus arctos.* These bears vary widely in size and color. The subspecies, or type, they call *Ursus arctos horribilis* is the grizzly bear of North America. This is the big brown bear of mainland Alaska, Canada, and the lower forty-eight states. Another subspecies of brown bear is the Kodiak, or Alaskan brown bear — *Ursus arctos middendorffi.* This is the bear that lives on Kodiak Island and the other smaller, coastal islands of Alaska. Kodiak bears are usually larger than grizzlies.

Relatives lived in Europe

These brown bears of North America are relatives of the great brown bears of Europe and Asia. They came to this continent thousands of years ago by crossing the land bridge, which it is believed, once connected Asia and Alaska. At first, they lived only in the far northern part of the continent. After the Ice Age, however, the grizzly bears roamed farther and farther. They moved southward as far as the mountains of Mexico. They went eastward throughout the plains country of the United States and Canada. Scientists believe they may have lived as far east as Ohio and Kentucky at one time. Grizzly bear skulls have also been found in southern Ontario and on the northern coast of Labrador.

The American Indians knew the grizzly bear well,

A drawing of a grizzly bear that was made in the late 1800's.

and they respected it. European explorers first began sighting it in the 1500's. The first explorer to write about the grizzly was Sebastian Vizcaino of Spain. In 1602, he reported grizzlies feeding on the carcass of a whale that had washed up on the beach in what is now the state of California. The first description of grizzly bears were not recorded until the Lewis and

Clark expedition of 1804-1806. Forty-three grizzlies were killed by members of this party during their journey across the western United States to the Pacific Ocean. They carefully recorded in their journal what they observed about the behavior of these bears.

Like the American Indians, these early explorers sensed the grizzly bear's power and strength. So did the fur trappers and mountain men who traveled the land. They all respected the grizzly. They stayed clear of the grizzly if possible, and defended themselves against it if necessary. The grizzly bears seemed to do the same.

Soon people began to settle the land. They marked off ranches to raise cattle and sheep. They fenced off land to grow crops of grain, vegetables, and fruit. Towns and cities grew up, and roads were built to connect them. The grizzly bear was pushed farther and farther back into the wilderness. The bears that did not retreat were killed. Two things now made humans more powerful than the grizzlies: guns and poisons.

Some grizzlies were killed for food. Some were killed out of fear. The settlers thought of the grizzly bear as a fierce beast. They had heard stories about how it hugged its victim to death, ate it alive, or buried it. So they killed these big brown bears before the bears could harm them, their families, or their livestock.

Grizzlies were also killed for sport. For more than a century, the bear was one of the most important big game animals on the North American continent. A grizzly was a prized trophy for many hunters. It still is hunted in Alaska, Canada, and the state of Montana, today.

A black grizzly feeds on blueberries west of Anchorage, Alaska.

Few grizzlies remain south of Canada

At one time, there may have been ten thousand or more grizzlies in the state of California alone. All of them had disappeared by 1924. It is believed that these were the largest of the grizzlies. Some of them may have weighed more than one thousand pounds. The smallest grizzlies were probably those that lived

Some grizzlies have weighed over one thousand pounds.

in the mountains of northern Mexico. These were extinct by the 1900's. The grizzly was extinct on the plains of the United States by the 1880's. It had vanished from the southwestern United States by the 1930's.

Today, grizzlies in the lower forty-eight states are found mainly in two places. They live in the region where the states of Montana, Idaho, and Wyoming join together. This is an area of about five million acres (2 million hectares). Yellowstone National Park is at the center of it. They also live in north-central Montana in a large area including the Scapegoat, Great Bear, and Bob Marshall wilderness areas. Glacier National Park is at the center of this three-and-a-half million acre (1.5 million hectare) region.

Scientists believe some grizzlies may also still live along the northern Idaho-Montana border and in the Selkirk mountains of northern Idaho and northeast Washington. Some may also live in the Cascade mountains in north-central Washington and in the San Juan mountains of northern Colorado. Once in a while a grizzly bear is seen in these scattered places.

No one is certain how many grizzlies there are today. There may be only seven to nine hundred of them remaining in the lower forty-eight states. Grizzly bears, however, are much more common in Alaska and Canada, where there is more unsettled wilderness.

CHAPTER TWO:

Long, shaggy fur

What makes most grizzly bears look different from other big brown bears is the color of their fur. Many have a white "frosting", on their fur which gives the bear an old, or "grizzled", look — and also its name.

The fur of the grizzly bear is long, thick, and shaggy. There is an underfur of very fine, soft hair. Over this fur lies long, coarse guard hairs. The grizzly often has a mane above its shoulders and upper back. This thick crop of guard hairs is sometimes called the roach. Beneath the chin, at the base of the jaw, the grizzly's hair may be even longer.

Grizzly bears shed their fur once a year in a process called its annual molt. This molting occurs during the late spring and early summer. The exact time of year depends on the weather where the bear lives. In general, a bear sheds its old fur sooner in warm climates. A grizzly bear can look quite ragged while it is molting.

New fur grows in to replace the old fur in late summer and early fall. The new fur is thicker and darker in color than the old fur that was shed. It is this new growth of fur that will keep the grizzly

The grizzly often has extra hair above its shoulders and under it's chin.

warm during the coming cold weather. In the summer, when it is warm, a thick coat is not needed.

White-tipped guard hairs

The color of the grizzly's coat varies widely from bear to bear. Some are pale buff and others are cinnamon colored. There are also bears that are dark brown or nearly black. The tips of the long guard hairs are white or blonde in color on some grizzlies. Bears that have a lot of this "frosting" are sometimes known as "silver tips".

Grizzlies that have a "frosted" look are known as "silver tips."

Not all grizzlies have this frosted look, however. This makes it difficult to tell whether a large brown bear in Alaska is a grizzly or a Kodiak. Sometimes, the only way to identify the bear is to look at its skull and its teeth. Not many people are able to do that!

The size and weight of grizzlies varies greatly from bear to bear. How big a grizzly is depends upon where it lives, the time of year, the amount of food there is, the bear's age, and its sex. As a rule, male grizzlies are larger than the females. Most adult males weigh from three hundred to one thousand pounds (136.4-455 kg). They are three to four feet (.9-1.2 m) tall at the shoulder. From nose to tail, they are about six to eight feet (1.8-2.5 m) long.

Captive grizzlies, such as those in zoos, may weigh more than one thousand pounds (455 kg). These bears are less active than grizzlies living free in the wild, so they are fatter. They may also be fed better food, and eat more often, than bears living in the wild.

In the past, the size and weight of the grizzly bear was often overstated. There were reports of bears weighing twenty-five hundred pounds (1.14 mt), standing twelve feet tall (3.7 m). Some reports were given by mountain men and hunters, who had felt the strength and power of the grizzly firsthand. Others were made by people who had viewed the animal only from afar. Who can blame them? There is no doubt that a thousand-pound (455 kg) bear is big. When it rears up on its hind feet to a height of eight or nine feet (2.5-3.0 m) and shows its teeth, it can seem even bigger!

A dished face

Like other brown bears, a grizzly has a large, broad head and a narrow jaw. Its face is "dished", something which sets it apart from the black bear. The black bear's face arches outward slightly. The grizzly's face arches inward like a dish.

The grizzly has a short neck, short rounded ears, and small dark eyes. Over its shoulders is a lump of muscle, which gives it a humped-shoulder appearance. The grizzly's tail is very short, almost buried in its fur coat. It has short, strong legs.

A plantigrade animal

Like all other bears, the grizzly's feet are plantigrade. This means it walks on the whole sole of the foot just like people do. The heel touches the ground with each step. Each foot has a heavy pad on the bottom. Each of its five toes has smaller pads. The sole of the foot is naked, with no hair between the pads. It is these pads that leave the imprint of the grizzly's foot. The tracks are often deep since the grizzly is such a heavy animal.

Some people think grizzlies are slow, clumsy animals, because of their huge bodies. Grizzlies do walk with a slow, steady shuffle. Yet they can go a long distance this way without stopping. When they want to, grizzly bears can gallop faster than a human can run. They have been clocked between forty and forty-five miles per hour (65-73 km/hr.). Grizzlies, however, cannot go very far at this speed.

Grizzly bears can also walk on their hind legs, but not for a very long time. If they sense danger they will often rear up to sniff the air.

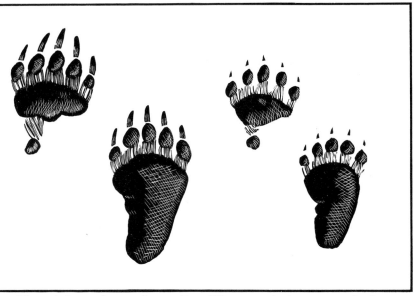

The picture above shows the difference between a grizzly paw mark (left) and a black bear's paw mark (right). Often, the black bear's shorter claws don't leave any marks.

Sharp claws and sense of smell

A grizzly bear has a long, curved claw extending from each of its toes. Its claws are much longer and wider than those of the black bear. They may be four to six inches (10-15 cm) long on its forefeet. These claws are usually longer than those on its hind feet. A grizzly bear's claws are light in color, sharp, and strong. They are non-retractile, which means that they cannot be pulled back in. The bear uses them when fighting. It also uses them for digging, for turning over rocks and logs, and for tearing things

Grizzlies have long, non-retractable claws.

apart. When young, the grizzly uses them to climb trees. As the bears grow older and heavier, however, they can no longer climb trees.

Unlike the claws of the black bear, the claws of an adult grizzly leave marks when it walks. These marks show in the grizzly bear's tracks.

Grizzly bears cannot see or hear very well. These two senses are not well-developed. Their sense of smell, however, is very sharp. They can smell food or humans from a long distance a way.

A smart, mean animal

Scientists consider the grizzly to be quite intelligent. It also has a very good memory.

As a rule, the grizzly bear is peaceful, sticks to its own territory, and minds its own business. It expects people to do the same. Yet the grizzly can be quite mean when defending its food or its young, or when it is hungry, wounded, or suddenly disturbed.

It is also difficult to predict how a grizzly bear is going to act. Bears make few sounds. They give no special warning before charging. With its great size, power and strength, the grizzly bear always deserves respect. It is one of the most dangerous wild animals in North America.

CHAPTER THREE:

Needs lots
of room

During the summer most of a grizzly bear's time is spent wandering over a large territory searching for food. This territory is called its home range. Grizzlies sleep wherever they can find a good spot. It may be a different place each day. The grizzly is an animal of the forest, although some grizzlies may be seen at times on the tundra of the far North.

Any animal as big as a grizzly bear needs a large home range. Male grizzlies tend to have larger home ranges than females. A female may have a range of only one hundred square miles (2.59 square km) or less. A male may have a range of one thousand square miles (2,500 square km) or more.

A home range will have all that a grizzly bear needs to live. Most important, it will have plenty of places to feed. A grizzly bear's home range is criss-crossed with paths between feeding places. The bear makes these paths by traveling the same route between feeding sites over and over again. A grizzly bear's home range may be bordered by other pathways, too. These border paths are used by many

The grizzly pauses among wild flowers.

A grizzly needs lots of room.

bears to get to seasonal feeding places that they all share — a rich berry field or a river filled with fish. A grizzly will use one part of its home range at a time, depending on the location of its food at different times of the year. If a grizzly can't find food, it may even shift the borders of its home range.

Grizzlies have a strong "homing" instinct. If scientists studying the grizzly capture a bear in one area and release it elsewhere, it can find its way back to its home range in a short time. Grizzlies do not usually defend their home ranges. In fact, some grizzly home ranges may even overlap.

Eats plants and animals

The grizzly bear is an omnivorous animal. This means it eats both plants and animals. Because it is the dominant animal in the land, it can prey on large animals. Yet it most often eats the small ones.

Whatever food it eats, the grizzly bear must have a lot of it. It takes a large amount of food to fuel the huge body of this bear! Often its meals come in small quantities, however. The search for food is never finished.

In the spring, grizzlies eat grass, leaves, roots, and moss. They overturn large rocks and small stones to find ants, beetles, crickets, and other insects. They tear apart logs and rotten trees to feast on grubs and larvae. Grizzlies like sweets, too. When summer comes, they will feed on fruit, wild berries of all kinds, and honey. Bee stings do not seem to bother them. In the fall, pine nuts, beechnuts, acorns, and other nuts are high on the list of favorite foods.

Grizzlies quite often kill small mammals, such as squirrels, gophers, and mice. The bigger, hoofed mammals, such as deer, are usually too quick for a bear. At times it may kill a sickly or careless deer.

Grizzlies that once lived on the plains of the United States fed upon the buffalo, a slower, hoofed mammal. Today's grizzlies can no longer do that since the buffalo is nearly extinct. Grizzlies today sometimes kill livestock on outlying ranches and farms. Cattle, sheep, hogs, and goats have all been prey for the grizzly.

Grizzlies sometimes feed on carrion, too. This is the kill of another animal. A carcass may be rotten, but the grizzly bear still eats it. A grizzly bear finds a carcass by following the scent. To help it locate the carcass, the grizzly may rear up on its hind legs and stretch its nose high into the air.

The search for food is a constant one, and the grizzly bear works hard. It does not wander aimlessly across its range. A grizzly knows when the snow will melt in different places, when and where the different plants will emerge, and when the berries will ripen. It follows these annual events high up into the mountains each summer and back down again in the fall. Along the way, animals of all kinds are caught whenever possible.

Although they are solitary animals most of the time, grizzlies will often feed in groups. The McNeil River in Alaska may host fifty grizzlies at night when the salmon are running in the fall. Such places draw bears from an entire region to feed. The bears return to these places year after year to eat their fill.

More than one grizzly may also feed on a carcass. The bear that finds it first usually eats its fill. Then it leaves the feast for others.

Grizzly bears also like garbage. They will travel quite a distance to feed at garbage dumps and trash sites, large and small.

As many as one hundred bears have been known to visit a large garbage dump in one night. Bears also return to these same places year after year to feed.

The grizzly bears eat as much as they can. They must store up enough fat during the summer and fall to last them through the winter months.

Mates in early summer

Spring and summer are the months for grizzly bear mating. Bears living where the weather warms early may mate from mid-May through mid-July. Those living in the north mate later.

Grizzly bears are polygamous, which means they often have more than one mate. They may even have several different mates in one day. Sometimes a male and female will pair off and stay together, but only for a very short while. The bond will not last at all if the male cannot defend the female from other interested males.

It is the larger, more aggressive males who mate with the females. The smaller, younger males may not mate until they are three or four years old. A

A young grizzly walks across the tundra.

This grizzly cub is three months old.

female grizzly usually does not mate until she is at least five years old. Those in colder climates may even be older when they have their first cubs.

A female grizzly continues to have cubs all her life, but she does not have a litter every year. Young females may have litters every other year. Older females often go three, four or more years between litters. This low birth rate is one of the reasons why there are so few grizzlies left.

Once they have mated, male and female grizzlies go their separate ways. They enjoy the rich summer's bounty, eating as much as they can before fall.

Sleeps during the winter

Grizzly bears sleep through most of the cold winter months in a den. They may sleep for five or six months. Scientists, however, do not call the grizzly bear's sleep a true hibernation. The grizzly's body temperature and heart rate remain about the same as they are during the rest of the year. Grizzlies will wake up if they are disturbed.

True hibernation occurs only when an animal's body temperature and heart rate decrease to a point where it cannot be awakened until spring. Scientists call the grizzly's long winter sleep a dormant period.

As a rule, a grizzly does not eat any food, drink

any water, or rid itself of any body wastes during its dormant period. The bear uses the energy from its layers of fat to stay alive. It stored this fat by eating large amounts of food in the late summer and fall.

Grizzly bears may retreat to their dens any time from early September until mid-November, depending upon the weather. As long as the weather stays warm, they stay outside. When the weather cools, the bears begin their winter sleep. The females are usually the first to enter their dens. Adult males are the last to go to sleep.

Grizzlies have been known to spend the winter in caves or hollow trees. Most of the time, however, they dig their dens in the ground. The den is usually on a steep slope. Such a place makes it easier for a bear to dig. It also provides good drainage for rain and melted snow. The entrance may be hidden behind bushes, but more often it is out in the open. Most entrances are on the side of the slope that is sheltered from winter winds. This helps keep out the cold. It also allows snow to build up on top of the den. A heavy snow cover helps to keep the den warm.

When it can, a grizzly will dig its den among the roots of trees or shrubs, or under large boulders or rocks. This helps to make the roof of the den stronger. A grizzly will dig a tunnel just big enough for it to crawl through. The tunnel may run straight back from the entrance, or it may angle up or down.

At the end of the tunnel, or off to one side, a grizzly digs a place that is slightly higher and wider. This spot is the actual den. It is like an underground room, or chamber. There is just enough space for the grizzly bear to stretch out and turn around.

A tunnel leads to the grizzlies den, which usually is not much larger than the bear itself.

Scientists used to think all grizzlies dug a new den each year. New research is showing that some grizzlies may use their dens year after year. Dens of older bears may be more elaborate than those of younger ones. There may be several chambers or more than one tunnel. The chamber may be lined with grass, roots, or tree boughs. As a grizzly bear grows older, it seems to learn how to make its den better. It can be quite a cozy place — for a bear.

Three grizzly cubs walk across a road in McKinley Park, Alaska.

Females raise the cubs

It is in her den that a female grizzly bear gives birth to her cubs. There may be only one cub or as many as four. Most often there is a litter of two or three. The cubs may be born any time from October to March.

A grizzly bear weighs less than a pound (30 g) at birth. From nose to tail it is less than twelve inches (3

cm) long. Its eyes and ears are closed, and it has no teeth and very little hair.

Not too much is known about a young cub's life in its mother's den. They sleep beside their mother and nurse at her nipples as she sleeps and awakens. The cubs may be quite active.

When spring comes, the cubs come out of the den with their mother. They stay with the female, continuing to nurse. The cubs may gain two hundred pounds (91 kg) during the first year of their life. They follow along behind their mother as she searches for food. The cubs bed down in the brush and leaves to sleep beside her. Bear cubs are very playful, romping in the grass and scampering up and down trees. A mother grizzly protects her young fiercely. As a rule, she quits nursing by fall, although sometimes the mother may nurse the cubs through their second winter.

Grizzly bear cubs usually stay with their mother in her den through their second winter. Some may even stay with their mother a third winter. The cubs are not fully grown for several years.

Awakens in the spring

As a rule, grizzlies stay in their dens each year until March, April, or May. Adult male grizzlies are the

Grizzlies come out of their dens in the spring.

A grizzly searches for food in the early spring.

first to leave. Females with cubs stay inside longer. Once again, the weather determines when they will leave their dens. Those living where the weather warms sooner, are the first to leave. Those living in colder climates stay inside longer.

It takes a few weeks for a grizzly bear to shake itself out of its long winter's sleep. They move slowly. Sometimes they must travel quite a distance from their den to find their first patch of green grass.

Scientists believe that the grizzly bears remember, from year to year, where the best feeding sites are. They also believe that grizzly bear cubs may learn from their mother where these places are and how to find them.

As more plants poke through the ground, the bears' appetites grow. By summer all are once again eating fully. All are fully active by then, too.

CHAPTER FOUR:

Grizzlies and people can't be together

What is to become of the grizzly bear in today's modern world?

Miners, loggers, oil drillers, ranchers, and road builders are pushing farther and farther back into the wilderness. So are campers, backpackers, hunters, and other people wanting to enjoy the wild, rugged land. People and grizzlies are bound to meet. The meeting may be in a berry patch some bright summer day. Or it may be on a hiking trail near a river filled with fish. It might be in a forest in the fall, when the pine nuts are at their fullest, or it might be in a clearing high up on some mountainside. No matter where it may happen, such meetings are not always in favor of either people or grizzlies. Too often the person who confronts a grizzly bear is badly hurt or killed. The grizzly bear, if it can be found, is often killed, too. This is to keep it from harming anyone else.

The greatest danger is from man-conditioned, grizzly bears. These are bears that have come into

Usually, waving the arms and yelling will scare-off a grizzly (top). If the bear keeps coming, it's best to play dead (bottom). Remember, no one can say for sure how to avoid an attack. It's best to stay away from a grizzly.

41

Once the grizzly loses its fear of people, it becomes dangerous.

contact with people in the past. Too often they have learned that such contact leads to food. They may have found a camper's food supply, or they may have uncovered some garbage. The people may be gone, but their scent lingers. These grizzlies lose their fear of people. They become more bold and more dangerous than ever.

Land preserved, bears protected

The grizzly bear's future seems secure in Alaska and Canada. Plenty of rugged wilderness still remains for it in these areas. In the lower forty-eight states, its future does not look as bright. Unless its habitat can be preserved and its life protected, the grizzly bears may not survive in this area.

The Wilderness Act of 1964 set aside millions of acres of land so that the natural habitat of many wild animals, including the grizzly bear, would be preserved. In 1975, the grizzly bear was also listed as a threatened species in the lower forty-eight states. This means that its life is now protected in that region. Yet if more die than are born each year, the bears still may not survive.

Their survival depends on people's respect for the grizzlies and their place in the wild. People may have to give up some of their progress and pleasures —

Grizzlies need wilderness areas to survive.

land development, hunting, camping, and hiking in backcountry wilderness areas. If people are not willing to do that, the grizzly bear could become extinct in the lower forty-eight states. No one will know when the last grizzly bear dies, or where it dies, or why. Some day, there just may not be any more wild grizzly bears to be seen, except in Alaska and Canada.

44

MAP:

The shaded areas
show where most
grizzlies are found
in North America.

INDEX/GLOSSARY:

WILDLIFE
HABITS & HABITAT

READ AND ENJOY THE SERIES:

THE
WHITETAIL • THE **PHEASANT**

THE
BALD EAGLE • THE **WOLVES**

THE
SQUIRRELS • THE **BEAVER**

THE
GRIZZLY • THE **MALLARD**

THE
RACCOON • THE **WILD CATS**

THE
RATTLESNAKE • THE **SHEEP**

THE
ALLIGATOR • THE **CARIBOU**

THE
CANADA GOOSE • THE **FOXES**